A Note to Parents and Teachers

Kids can imagine, kids can laugh and kids can learn to read with this exciting new series of first readers. Each book in the Kids Can Read series has been especially written, illustrated and designed for beginning readers. Humorous, easy-to-read stories, appealing characters, and engaging illustrations make for books that kids will want to read over and over again.

To make selecting a book easy for kids, parents and teachers, the Kids Can Read series offers three levels based on different reading abilities:

Level 1: Kids Can Start to Read

Short stories, simple sentences, easy vocabulary, lots of repetition and visual clues for kids just beginning to read.

Level 2: Kids Can Read with Help

Longer stories, varied sentences, increased vocabulary, some repetition and visual clues for kids who have some reading skills, but may need a little help.

Level 3: Kids Can Read Alone

Longer, more complex stories and sentences, more challenging vocabulary, language play, minimal repetition and visual clues for kids who are reading by themselves.

With the Kids Can Read series, kids can enter a new and exciting world of reading!

POLICE OFFICERS

With thanks to the Metropolitan Toronto Police and
to the Honourable Madame Justice Donna G. Hackett — P.B.

With thanks to the RCMP Sechelt Detachment and for
my Dad PC 260 LaFave (Ret.) — K.L.

Acknowledgments
Thanks to Senior Officer Mike Lawson, Maureen Skinner Weiner and the
Metropolitan Toronto Police Service for their review of the revised text.

 Kids Can Read is a trademark of Kids Can Press Ltd.

Kids Can Press acknowledges the financial support of the Government of Ontario,
through the Ontario Media Development Corporation's Ontario Book Initiative; the
Ontario Arts Council; the Canada Council for the Arts; and the Government of
Canada, through the BPIDP, for our publishing activity.

Published in Canada by   Published in the U.S. by
Kids Can Press Ltd.   Kids Can Press Ltd.
29 Birch Avenue   2250 Military Road
Toronto, ON M4V 1E2   Tonawanda, NY 14150

www.kidscanpress.com

Edited by David MacDonald
Designed by Kathleen Collett
Educational consultant: Maureen Skinner Weiner, United Synagogue Day School,
Willowdale, Ontario
U.S. reviewer: Senior Officer Mike Lawson, Germantown, New York
Canadian reviewer: Metropolitan Toronto Police Service
Printed in China by WKT Company Limited

The hardcover edition of this book is smyth sewn casebound.
The paperback edition of this book is limp sewn with a drawn-on cover.

CM 04 0 9 8 7 6 5 4 3 2 1
CM PA 04 0 9 8 7 6 5 4 3 2 1

National Library of Canada Cataloguing in Publication Data
Bourgeois, Paulette
Police officers / written by Paulette Bourgeois ; illustrated by Kim
LaFave.

(Kids Can read)
First published under title: Canadian police officers.
ISBN 1-55337-742-7 (bound). ISBN 1-55337-743-5 (pbk.)

1. Police — Juvenile literature. I. LaFave, Kim II. Title. III. Series: Kids Can read
(Toronto, Ont.)

HV8138.B595 2004   j363.2   C2003-907467-6

Kids Can Press is a *Corus*™ Entertainment company

POLICE OFFICERS

Paulette Bourgeois • Kim LaFave

Kids Can Press

Clank, clang, clatter, bang!

Natalie hears noises and she's worried. Someone has been stealing bicycles on her street. Maybe the thieves are in her garage! Natalie creeps into her parents' room. "Call the police," she whispers.

Natalie's mother reaches for the phone.
The police number is by the phone.
"We think somebody is trying to break in,"
she tells the police. "Our name is Best.
We live at 123 Main Street. The closest
intersection is Main and South streets."

"The police will be right here," she
tells Natalie.

The police dispatcher gets the call. The dispatcher sends a message to the police car closest to Natalie's house.

The officers hear the message. They are on the way! The officers do not use their siren this time. They want to arrive quietly and catch the thieves in action.

The officers search the area. All they find is a garbage can that has been knocked over.

"There have been a lot of bicycle thefts around here," the officers tell the Best family. "Do you have a good lock on your bike?"

Natalie nods. "And I wrote down the kind of bike I have and the serial number," she says.

"That's smart!" say the officers. "Sometimes we find lost or stolen bicycles and we don't know who owns them."

On the way to school, Natalie notices
something unusual. There is a big blue
van parked behind an empty building.
She writes the van's plate number in her
notebook and tells the principal when she
gets to school. The principal calls the police.

The officers drive slowly by the
schoolyard. At the bike rack, they see
two men look around nervously.
Then, in a flash, the men slice through
a bicycle lock with a small saw.

Before the two men can drive away, the
police officers say, "You're under arrest for
stealing. You're
coming with us to
the police station."

At the station, the men are taken to a
room to be questioned. They can ask to
have lawyers with them. The police officers
who made the arrest still have work to do.
They look in the back of the blue van.
There are 15 bicycles inside!

The men are let go until their trial in a courtroom.

At the trial, a judge and two lawyers are in the courtroom. One lawyer helps the two men tell their side of the story. The other lawyer helps the police present their side of the story.

The judge decides if the men are guilty of stealing bicycles. If they are guilty, the judge will tell the men what their punishment will be.

Later that night, Natalie hears *clank, clang, clatter, bang!*

"The bike thieves are back!" she calls to her parents. "Call the police!"

The officers arrive within seconds. They move quickly and quietly through the dark. They shine their flashlights into the alley.

"I've caught the masked robbers," says the officer. "But I think I'll let them go with a warning."

A police officer has to be prepared for anything.

Facts about Police Officers

All police officers are ready to help
people who are lost, hurt or afraid. There
are many different kinds of police work.
Some officers teach children to be safe.

Some officers control the crowds
at concerts and sports events.

Some officers investigate crimes and
traffic accidents by finding out what
happened.

Police officers who wear uniforms patrol by car, walk on foot, ride a horse or even patrol by bicycle.

Sometimes police may try to catch criminals by wearing regular clothes and pretending they are not police officers. This kind of police work is called "undercover."

in a van

in a helicopter

on a motorcycle

in a boat

on a bicycle

in a patrol car

Police officers are physically fit. They are not too short and not too tall. They must have good eyesight. Police officers have guns but they hope they never have to use them.

Some officers wear bulletproof vests.
They carry notebooks and handcuffs
and wear a belt with a nightstick and
a flashlight.

Ways to Stay Safe

Always use the same route for going to and from school, playgrounds and friends' homes. Make sure your parents know the routes you take.

Make sure your parents know where you are all the time.

Always say "No" if a stranger invites you into his or her home or car.

Make sure you know the phone number for the police.

Always tell your parent or an adult you trust if something has happened that bothers you. You don't have to keep it a secret no matter what anyone says.

Always keep the door locked when you are home alone.

Always pretend you've got grown-up company if you're home alone.

Always have a family password. Adults who want you to stay with them, or go somewhere with them, must know the password.

Always refuse to go anywhere with a stranger or somebody who makes you feel uncomfortable. Most people are helpful and kind, but some people might try to trick you. They might offer you something nice such as a toy or an ice cream. They might even tell you that something is wrong with your parents.

Never go anywhere with a stranger.

Remember to always be alert and stay safe!